David Drizzledrop

AND THE

Puddle

Party

WRITTEN BY ELAYNE HEANEY

ILLUSTRATED BY PAULA REEL

To David,
You finally got your own wonderful character in a book!
I hope you'll love it forever xx

Written and Concept by Elayne Heaney
wonderfullyweatherybooks@gmail.com

Illustrations and Design by Paula Reel
paulreel@gmail.com

Special thanks to Copy Editors
Liz Hudson
liz@littleredpen.com
Natasha McBhaird
natashamaca@gmail.com

Printed by GPS Colour, Belfast
www.GPScolour.co.uk

First Printing, 2021

ISBN 978-1-5272-9813-2

Published by Wonderfully Weathery Books
Dublin

wonderfullyweatherybooks@gmail.com

David Drizzledrop, come out to play!
Will you bring us your sprinkles today?
Bring us some showers and
lots of rain too?
We'll put on our wellies and
splash about with you!

Meet **DAVID DRIZZLEDROP**,
he is a drizzledrop called David.
He lives in a place called Weatherville,
where it's
COOL AND SHADED.

Inside the clouds is where he'll be,
living **HAPPILY** with his family.

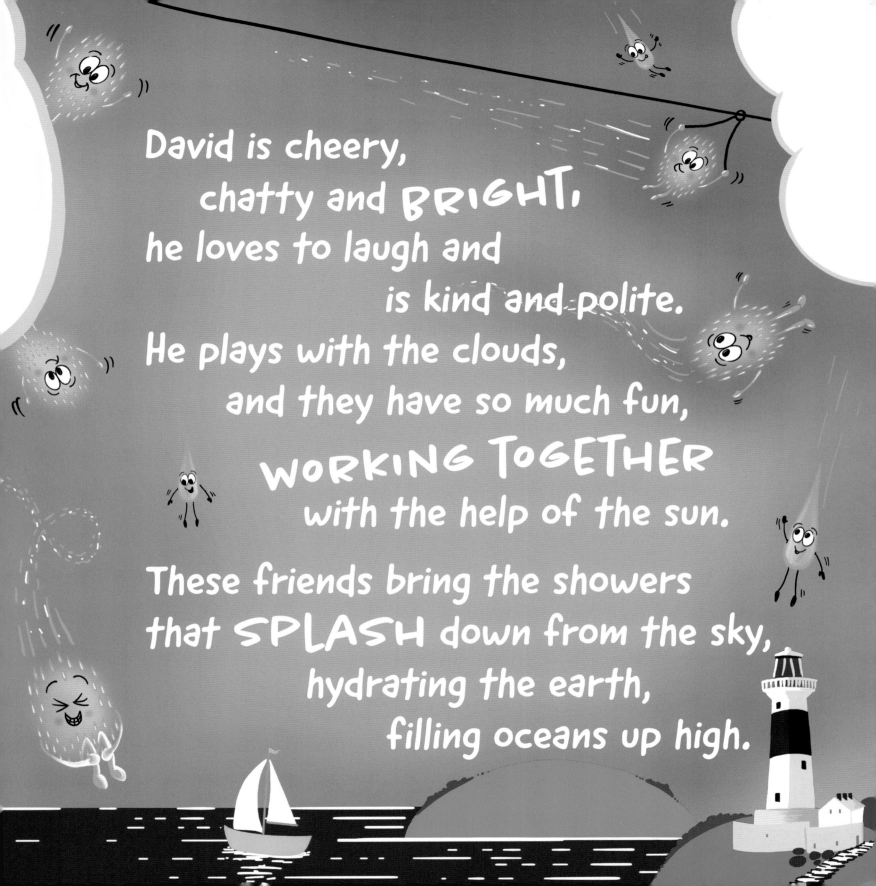

David is cheery,
chatty and BRIGHT,
he loves to laugh and
is kind and polite.
He plays with the clouds,
and they have so much fun,
WORKING TOGETHER
with the help of the sun.

These friends bring the showers
that SPLASH down from the sky,
hydrating the earth,
filling oceans up high.

Drizzledrops and raindrops
FLY THROUGH THE AIR,
landing on cars, on grass and
on people's hair!
They're not always welcome
with the humans below,
who run for umbrellas when
the drops shout
`HELLO!'

David's friend Ricky
is a water drop too –
he is a **RAINDROP**
ready to jump down on you.

Ricky is friendly, brave in every way,
and he looks for **ADVENTURES**
every single day.

One day Ricky's invited
to a **PUDDLE** party below
and asks his friend David
            if he would like to go.
Ricky is excited for this happy news,

but David looks **NERVOUS**
and shakes in his shoes.
This is the first time
he'll **JUMP** without Mum,
he's scared of falling
and landing on his bum.

All the drops gather and
make the clouds turn grey,
then start to TICKLE
their friends in a giddy
kind of way.

The clouds laugh so hard
their bellies start to hurt,
and they
SQUEEZE OUT THE DROPS
with a push and a spurt.

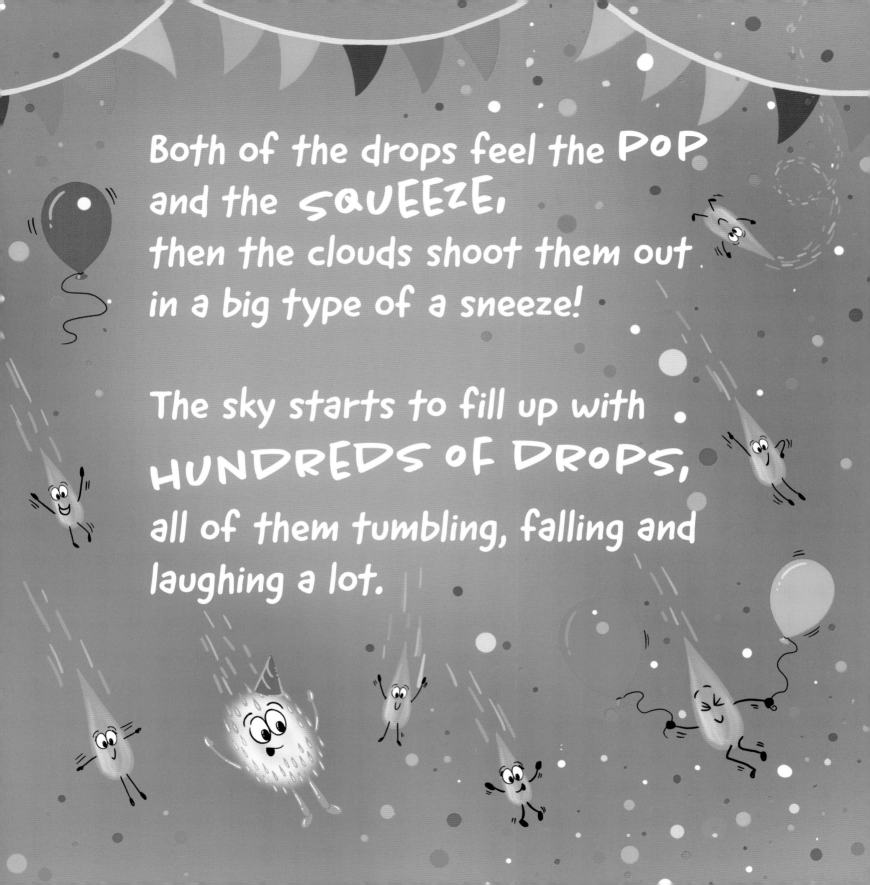

Both of the drops feel the POP
and the SQUEEZE,
then the clouds shoot them out
in a big type of a sneeze!

The sky starts to fill up with
HUNDREDS OF DROPS,
all of them tumbling, falling and
laughing a lot.

David is brave,
and he flies through the air,
and
SAILS THROUGH THE SKY
with style and with flair.

Why was he scared of going it alone?
he would have GONE SOONER
if he only had known!

As raindrops and drizzledrops
fall to the ground,
a **LARGE PUDDLE** forms
which is big, wide and round.
Everyone's **SPLASHING**
and giggling away,
ready to have fun
on this amazing day.
The older drops begin some
SWIMMING RACES,
and the younger ones cheer them
with smiles on their faces.

PADDLING PUDDLE

There's sliding and DIVING
and cannonballs tricks,
as the drops swim about
with plenty of kicks.

They party all day and **HAVE SO MUCH FUN,** but the puddle starts evaporating from the heat of the sun.

As the sky above brightens,
the temperature starts to CHANGE,
and one by one the water drops
        start to FEEL STRANGE.
The sun heats them up,
which turns them to steam,
and they feel like they're FLOATING,
                as if in a dream.

The wind blows them
to the COLD AIR up high,
as they turn back into water drops
soaring up in the sky.

David and Ricky land back in Weatherville, ready to tell their friends of their very big **THRILL.** David tells his Mum about his adventure that day, and she happily hugs him in her very special way.

welcome to Weatherville

So next time you see a fluffy cloud up high, you'll know it's full of drops waiting to jump into **THE SKY.**

THE WATER CYCLE

WHAT IS THE WATER CYCLE?

Water on Earth is everywhere and it's constantly moving. It is recycled and used over and over again – this recycling process is called The Water Cycle. Let's take a closer look!

PRECIPITATION

When clouds get heavy and full of water drops these drops pop out of the clouds and fall to the ground in the form of rain, drizzle or even snow!

EVAPORATION

These water drops land in seas, lakes, ponds and puddles – when the sun shines it heats them up and they and turn into water vapour. This process is called Evaporation. Did you ever see your grown-up boil a kettle? Watch the steam rise when the water heats up!

CONDENSATION

These water vapours travel up into the sky and meet the cold air – this cold causes them to cool down and turns them back into water drops again. These drops bundle together to form clouds and then the whole cycle starts all over again!